As they grow bigger and heavier some of the plants have to be tied up with ropes to stop them falling over. The banana plants need lots of water to grow in this heat. Can you see where they get it from?

These bananas are big enough to cut now. They are still green and unripe but they have a long journey ahead. Because bananas get bruised and damaged easily, the men put plastic bags round them to stop spiders and fruit bats, birds and animals nibbling at them as they grow.

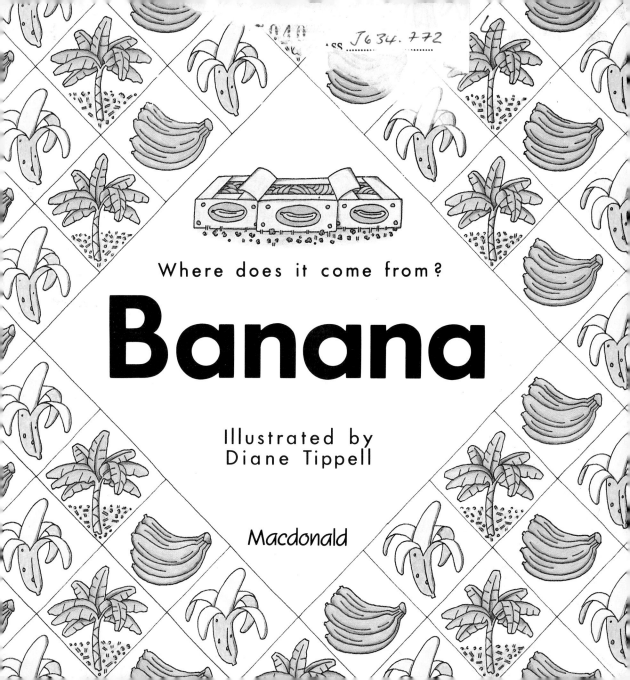

Where does it come from?

Banana

Illustrated by
Diane Tippell

Macdonald

This is where bananas come from: big farms in some of the hottest countries in the world. They take about a year to grow. First a root is planted. It grows leaves, then a flower and later, little green bananas sprout from the flower stem.

Now they are cutting the heavy stems off the tree the men are very careful not to bump them — so careful they don't even put them down. They hang them up on a wire and pull them along to the packing station by tractor.

The people working here at the packing station clean and pack the bananas. Some take the bags off, cut the bunches of fruit off the big stems and put them in a tank to wash any dirt or insects off. Others take them out again, break them into smaller bunches and put them on a moving belt to be rinsed. Any bruised or damaged bananas are thrown away at once.

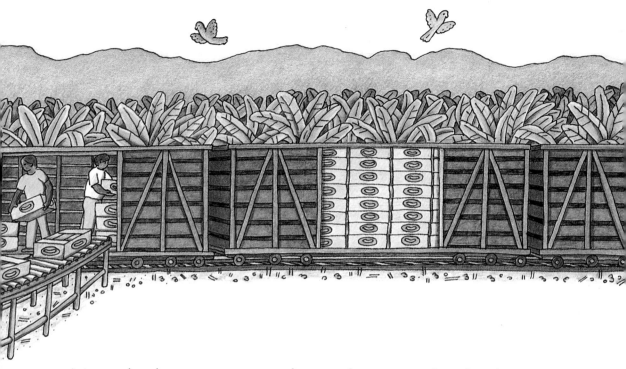

Now the bananas are clean, they are checked, labelled and packed in cardboard boxes. The full boxes are loaded straight into railway wagons to take them to the ship which will carry them across the sea. Can you see the gaps in the side of the wagons? These let the air in. From now on it's very important that the bananas are kept cool so that they don't ripen before they get to the end of their journey.

The train has reached the port and the men who work at the docks have loaded the boxes of bananas into the holds of this ship. Now it is setting out across the sea. The journey can take two weeks or more, and all the time the bananas must not get too hot or too cold. Huge fans pump air along big pipes to the holds all day and all night. And in the engine room the ship's engineers have a special control panel. Can you find it? The engineer is adjusting the fans to keep the temperature of the air just right.

Now the ship has arrived. It's too cold to grow bananas here —that's why they have to be brought from so far away. The boxes must be unloaded quickly or the bananas will get chilled. The dockers pile them on to pallets for the cranes to lift out, then the forklift truck drivers whisk them away into big lorries. Some of the boxes are opened. Are the bananas all right? The quality controllers check them before the lorries take them off to be ripened.

This is the place where the bananas are allowed to ripen at last. They come in green and go out yellow! The manager is checking the ones which have just arrived from the docks. Then they are shut into those giant cupboards and warm air and special gas are pumped in to ripen them.

Can you see the bananas being taken out and checked again? These ones have been ripening for 5 days and they're starting to turn yellow. They are ready to sell now so they are going off to the supermarket on the smaller van.

When the banana van arrives it is still early and the supermarket isn't open yet. But things are busy at the back door of the shop. The van driver unloads the boxes and takes them inside.

Now the people who work in the shop unpack the bananas, weigh them and stick a price tag on each bunch ready to sell. And all the time the bananas are getting riper and yellower.

The supermarket is soon full of people when it opens. John
and Ellie and their dad are buying food for the week. They
already have a lot in their trolley but John wants some
bananas.

Better put them on top of the load to make sure they don't get squashed! The shop assistant brings more bananas from the store room to put on the shelves. They don't seem to stay there for long.